C000165971

Natascha Schnelder-Bouman

the **African Grey Parrot**

A guide to selection, housing, care,
nutrition, behaviour, health and breeding

about pets

Contents

Foreword

This book is addressed to those people who are
planning to purchase an African Grey Parrot, those who
have just purchased one and all those who would like
to know more about this intelligent, smart parrot
species. The African Grey Parrot is one of the parrots
most commonly kept in captivity (aviculture).

The themes of this book include origins of the African
Grey Parrot, buying, caging and care. Feeding, health,
behaviour and breeding are also featured, of course.

Natascha Snelder-Bouman has been breeding a
number of dwarf and large parrot species, including the
African Grey, for years. Since 1995, she has also been
chief editor of Pakara Magazine, a twice-monthly Dutch
publication for lovers, owners and breeders of big
parrots, amazons, cockatoos and macaws. This
function has also enabled her to learn about other
people's knowledge and experience in keeping and
breeding parrots.

The earlier publication in the About Pets series, "The
Parrot", draws a general picture of all large parrot
species. This book now casts a specific look at the
wishes and needs of the African Grey Parrot.

About Pets

about pets

A Publication of About Pets.

All rights reserved, including the right to
reproduce this book or portions
thereof in any form whatsoever.

Copyright © 2003
About Pets
co-publisher United Kingdom
Kingdom Books
PO9 5TL, England

ISBN 1852792000
First printing December 2004
Second revised printing Januar 2006

Original title: de grijze roodstaart
© 2004-2006 Welzo Media Productions
bv, Warffum, the Netherlands
www.aboutpets.info

Photos:
Natascha Snelder-Bouman,
Rob Dekker,
Jessie Claire van Breederode Galligo

Printed in China

The African Grey Parrot originates in Africa and it can still be admired in the wild there. The African Grey Parrot can be found in western and central Africa, sometimes even in Kenya.

Origins

They can even be found on the lower slopes of Kilimanjaro. They can be found in basically all countries within 10 degrees north and south of the equator. The parrot's natural habitat consists of woodlands, mangroves and savannas, but it can also be found in agricultural areas, as fields offer easy access to food. The African Grey is limited to lowlands and is found at the highest at 2200 metres in mountainous regions.

In Africa, the bird lives mostly in large groups of several hundred birds. It is a very sociable creature and these birds do everything together: sleep, search for food, play and drink. Living in a group provides security. Couples find each other in the group and only separate from it during the mating season. The partners will stay together throughout their lives, and the bond between them is very strong.

African Greys are very vocal birds which communicate a lot with each other. In the morning hours they let each other know where they are going to forage for food, and in the evening they communicate when they find their partners and settle down to sleep. They also call to each other whilst flying.

In general

the **African Grey Parrot**

Other African parrot species

There are more parrot species in Africa than just the Grey. Here are some of the better known species:

- Meyer's Parrot (*Poicephalus meyeri*)
- Senegal Parrot (*Poicephalus senegalus*)
- Red-fronted Parrot or Jardine's Parrot (*Poicephalus gulielmi*)
- Cape Parrot (*Poicephalus robustus* and *Poicephalus fucicollis*)
- Greater and Lesser Vasa Parrot (*Coracopsis Vasa* and *Coracopsis Nigra*)

Lovebirds, a group of colourful, cheerful dwarf parrots, also originate on this continent.

Subspecies

The African Grey Parrot has the Latin, scientific, name of *Psittacus erithacus*. This means something similar to 'parrot with some red on it'. It is always useful to know the Latin name of your bird. It is used by official authorities and is helpful in correspondence with foreigners, as it is the same throughout the world. Anyone will know exactly which species you are talking about.

Psittacus erithacus has the following subspecies. You can recognise a subspecies by the third Latin word in its name:
- *Psittacus erithacus erithacus* – Congo Grey Parrot

- *Psittacus erithacus timneh* - Timneh Grey Parrot

Whether the occasionally mentioned subspecies *Psittacus erithacus* princeps actually exists is doubtful. Expert opinions differ on this matter. According to one opinion, it is an official subspecies with distinct characteristics, whereas others find the differences too small to talk of a separate subspecies. The critics regard it as a regional colour difference of the plumage. The leading German publication 'Papageien' and other bodies concerned with big parrots erased the *princeps* from their lists some

Senegal Parrot

Lesser Vasa Parrot

Timneh Grey Parrot

Grey Parrot is the most common African Grey in Europe. These birds are approximately 33 to 40 cm, have a primarily grey plumage with light red tailfeathers, a black beak, naked white cheeks, dark grey legs and black nails. The plumage can be of various shades of grey, and can differ a lot between individual birds.

Psittacus erithacus timneh

The Timneh Grey Parrot was first discovered and named by a Mr Fraser. The Timneh looks like the Congo variety, but is a lot smaller, slimmer and lighter (27 to 32 cm). The grey plumage is often darker than that of the Congo variety and the tailfeathers are more brown-red than light red. The upper part of the beak is horn coloured instead of black. The habitat of the Timneh is limited to Liberia, Sierra Leone, the Ivory Coast, Kenya and Uganda. The Timneh Grey Parrot is less often found in captivity than its Congo cousin. A lot of birds have been captured and remain very shy.

Left and middle: Timneh Grey Parrot
Right: Congo Grey Parrot

time ago. This is why this subspecies will not be covered any further in this book, and this bird is also hardly ever found in captivity. The differences between Congo and Timneh Grey Parrots are, however, very obvious, and will be described further in this book. The pictures also aim to make the differences more obvious.

Appearance

Psittacus erithacus erithacus

This is called the 'nominal form', the main form of this species. It was first discovered and recorded by a Mr Linné in 1758. The Congo

Young African Greys

Young African Greys can be recognised by their dark eyes. To begin with, the Iris is very dark grey (almost black), but it lightens up gradually until it eventually turns (light) yellow. The tailfeathers are also a darker red when the bird is younger. Bear this in mind if you really want to be sure that you are purchasing a young bird.

Natural enemies

The African Grey's natural enemies consist of birds of prey, apes and other tree climbers who are particularly keen on the eggs. Besides this, African Greys are also very popular as pets, which means that they are still being captured in large numbers. Although the bird has not yet been recognised by the IUCN (International Union for the Conservation of Nature) as an endangered species, its numbers are decreasing quite quickly due to illegal trade and the destruction of its habitat and nesting opportunities. Illegal trade is the biggest problem, as the natives regard catching the birds as an important source of income. Thankfully, African Greys breed very well in captivity, which makes the import of captured birds superfluous.

The BUDEP law

The Congo Grey Parrot is being bred substantially in captivity. As mentioned above, it is therefore not necessary to import them to Europe from the wild. If you want to buy a parrot, check that it has a solid ring as a sign that it has been bred in captivity. This is very important, especially as the laws concerning foreign animal species are becoming stricter by the day. All parrot species, except the budgerigar and the cockatiel, are protected by the law covering endangered foreign animal and plant species, the so-called BUDEP law. You need a keeper's permit for rare species. For more common species, such as the African Grey, the law says that you are only allowed to own an animal if you can prove that it has been bred in captivity (except in some special circumstances). A solid, seamless, ring proves this, as it can only be fitted onto a young chick's leg.

- No paperwork is necessary if birds are kept and sold within the EU only.
- Paperwork does become necessary if birds are bought from or sold to a non-EU country.

Identification

It is important to be able to identify a parrot. There are several methods.

Solid ring

A solid, seamless, ring (without a weld or opening) can only be fitted on a young chick (of approximately three weeks) and it is the only proof of the bird having been bred in captivity. On the ring are the details of the bird society which issued the ring, the year when it was fitted, the breeder's number and the serial number of the bird. This means that each ring has a unique code enabling you to trace the origins of each bird. This plays an important role when breeding, for example. If a new bird seems to come from the same breeder as the one you would like to mate it with, then it is advisable to check that they are not related. Mating unrelated birds is best. Only if certain 'family' characteristics are to be enhanced in future generations should a breeder mate birds from the same family. Too much in-breeding (mating of related birds) is unhealthy, however, as it will weaken chicks of future generations.

There is also international legislation concerning endangered animal species: CITES (Convention on International Trade in Endangered Species of wild fauna and flora). The most endangered animals are registered on the CITES list I, the slightly less endangered species on list II. The African Grey is on the CITES list II, together with many other parrot species. Some important consequences of placing a parrot on list II are:

- These species can be kept and traded freely within the EU with or without rings.
- Formally, one must prove that a non-ringed bird has been imported legally. In practice, owners of a single bird will hardly ever be prosecuted for this.

If you breed African Greys yourself, ensure that all young chicks are fitted with a solid ring. Not only is it obligatory, but it also means that your birds will always be identifiable and traceable.

'Open' ring

An 'open' ring is a ring which is not entirely closed. It can be attached to the bird at any time (it is just layed round the leg and pressed closed). It does not make a difference whether the bird is young or old and whether it has been bred in captivity or been caught in the wild and imported. An 'open' ring is therefore no proof that the bird was born in captivity. Whether the ring is around the right or the left leg does not indicate the bird's sex, although a lot of people will tell you otherwise.

If you would like more information about the BUDEP law and its consequences, you can contact the CITES office. The address can be found in the chapter 'Useful contacts'.

Electronic chip

An electronic chip is a great means of identification. A chip can also be implanted into an adult bird at any time. This does mean, however, that a chip is no proof that a bird was born in captivity. On the plus side, a chip is very useful when a bird has been stolen or has gone missing, as, contrary to a ring, you cannot remove a chip. If a lost bird is found, you can prove your ownership by the chip number. This is often the only proof of ownership if the ring has been removed or lost.

Photographs

Photographs of your African Grey can be supporting 'evidence' if your bird has been lost or stolen. The ring and chip are still the most important means of identification, but in some cases pictures of the bird can be a helpful addition. Your parrot must, however, have some obvious marks, such as missing nails, an abnormal beak, an unusually coloured plumage, etc. As already mentioned, a photograph will never substitute the number on a solid ring or on an electronic chip.

If you have never owned an African Grey, but are seriously considering buying one, then here are some tips.

How old should it be?

Most people see it as an advantage to form a strong bond with a handreared, tame bird. There are, however, a lot of young parrots for sale, which have been reared by their parents. They make just as good pets! It might take a little more attention to tame them, but experience shows that a young African Grey will normally become totally tame within a few days. A lot of chicks therefore stay with their parents until they are ten to eleven weeks old, at which time they can be brought into the house. After about twelve to thirteen weeks, the chicks can go to their new homes.

Mental strength

A young African Grey of ten to eleven weeks will be quite strong and have quite a bit of plumage. The most important thing, however, is that it will also have developed quite a lot mentally. This means that the animal is psychologically quite strong and can cope much better with being moved from its familiar dark nest to a big light room. It is of course for good reason that young African Greys fledge when they are approximately thirteen weeks old. They are then old enough to leave the nest of their own free will and to explore their environment. Their ability to learn and their inquisitive nature draws them outside and their horizon expands rapidly. Of course, they also learn to fly, eat by themselves, play, socialise with other birds and to

Buying your parrot

cope with unexpected circumstances and changes.

If you do not have the necessary expertise, never buy a young African Grey that has to be reared by hand. A few weeks later, the bird will be able to eat by itself, and this is the right moment to take it home. This wait will not compromise how tame the bird will become. African Greys become indpendent at twelve to thirteen weeks. This does not mean that they no longer like their baby food, but it means that they are able to eat on their own.

Captured or born in captivity?

There is a huge difference between birds which have been caught and imported, and those pets which have been reared by breeders. If you intend to keep birds as pets, then you should avoid a captured bird. These birds are used to a life in the wild and are often so badly traumatised and weakened by their journey that they will never recover from this experience. It is almost always impossible to tame such birds. They are also often fully grown and therefore find it very difficult to adapt to a life in captivity. Captured birds do not have rings and are often extremely shy and nervous.

If you want a pet bird, always choose one which has been born in captivity, whether it has been

reared by its parents or by hand. You can get to know the bird as a young chick in its nest or in the breeder's house.

Choosing your parrot

Be aware of the following points when choosing a young bird:
- The first point to bear in mind is choosing the right breeder. The relationship has to be based on liking each other and good communication. Ask knowledgeable people to recommend a good breeder to you. Never buy a bird on impulse, via the classified section in your local newspaper, via the internet, through a middle-man or from a vendor you do not know.

- Ask a lot of questions and keep asking. Ask about anything you can think of and that you would like to know more about. An involved breeder will be happy to tell you anything you want to know and more.
- Read as much as possible about the species you have chosen. About advantages and disadvantages, feeding, space, noise level, etc.
- Ask to see the parent animals. It is particularly nice if parents and chicks are together. Then you know for sure that the bird has been bred by the breeder himself.
- Do not take the bird home the first time you see it. Allow yourself time to think about it (even if you find it difficult) and make a new appointment with the breeder once you are certain that you want to buy the bird. There are also breeders who do not sell their youngsters to the first person that comes along. They want to make sure that you have seriously considered all the pros and cons.
- Do not buy the 'sad' bird. A parrot will keep an illness hidden as long as possible (also see the chapter 'Health'). Any sign of illness in the wild is a sign of weakness, which enemies, of course, pick up straight away. Any bird knows this instinctively and will therefore try and disguise any signs of illness as long as possible. A bird which

looks sad and unwell is therefore probably very ill.
- When you pick up the bird, ask the breeder for some food. Feed this to your bird for the first few days, and then you can decide if you want to (gradually) change the food.
- Bear in mind the price of the bird. Parrots can be a very expensive purchase, but this is not all. You also have to reserve a substantial amount of money for its living quarters and food. By choosing in advance whether you would like a cage or an aviary you will become aware of the total costs. Vets' fees can also be an important factor (e.g. for the vetting).
- Figure out what to do when you go on holiday: find potential 'parrot-sitters', places where it can stay, find out where you can take it with you, etc.
- Plan not only for your present living arrangements, family and working hours, but also for the future. An African Grey will accompany you for a good 30 to 50 years! Of course, nobody can be expected to plan that far ahead, but maybe you should take a moment to consider that you are not buying a dwarf hamster which will only live for 3 years. There are many people who mention their parrot in their will, so that the future of their darling is secured if they should die first.

Purchase contract

Make arrangements with the vendor about having the bird checked over (vetted) by a vet specialising in birds. The vet can do a thorough examination to evaluate and check the bird. Together with the vet, you can decide which examinations, tests and checks should be part of the vetting.

To prevent disappointments and misunderstandings, it is important to write down any agreements with the breeder. This can be a purchase contract, where you can mention the following: details of buyer and breeder; ring number and maybe chip number of the bird; species; details of the vetting; agreed tests; resolutive conditions of the purchase; splitting of costs of any examinations. Also check in the chapter 'Useful Contacts'.

Quarantine

If you already have birds, you should keep the new bird separate for a while. You can then observe it and wait for the test results. The new bird can get used to its new surroundings. Getting it used to new food is also easier this way. Your existing group of birds will not be in danger in case the new one does appear to have a disease after all.

An adequate quarantine should last for six to eight weeks or even

the **African Grey Parrot**

What it should look like
Here are a few pointers that will help you choose a healthy bird. A
  healthy parrot should not:
- crouch with feathers sticking out
- sleep constantly while people are standing in front of its cage
- breathe audibly (gasping or wheezing)
- let its tail whip in the rhythm of its breathing
- let its wings droop
- have lice or feather mites on or under its feathers
- sleep on the ground

A healthy parrot should:
- display a nice plumage, laying smoothly against its body
- clean its feathers regularly
- have shiny eyes
- have dry nostrils without discharge or crusts
- keep its beak closed when resting
- keep an eye on its surroundings
- have a clean anus
- eat independently
- sit on a perch and sleep on one leg
- have a smooth and clean beak

the **African Grey Parrot**

longer if the test results are not back yet or if other circumstances dictate that the bird should be kept apart for longer. This might seem excessive, but especially if you have many other birds, animals that you are particularly fond of or which are of high value, a quarantine of that one new bird means you are protecting all the others. And that can be worth a lot more than the costs of those few extra tests. Any preventative measures when buying a new bird are therefore in the interest of all your birds!

Joining a club or society

All buyers of an African Grey should really become members of a bird club or society. You can become a member of a nationwide or a local society to stay in touch with all new developments, to learn from each others' experience and to have somewhere you can go with your questions if you are encountering problems. Most societies consist of very active members who all have the same interest at heart: birds. Club evenings and activities are all directed towards their hobby and result in useful (and sociable) contacts. These can be particularly helpful in emergencies or when you are facing new situations. It should all be for your and your bird's benefit.

Published information

You should not underestimate magazines and books as sources of useful information. Many bird clubs or societies have in-house publications, which will become accessible to you as a member. There are also plenty of books concerning your hobby. You can fill your bookshelf to your heart's content with books about parrots in general and African Greys in particular. Check out the availability of parrot books in your local library.

The internet also offers a lot of information about the Grey and all other parrots. This is very useful on the one hand, but, on the other, anyone can publish anything on the internet. Therefore always be very critical with information, check if you can make out the 'author' and, if in doubt, always check with others. Especially when buying or selling a bird, it pays to be extra vigilant.

In Europe today, some countries, including the Netherlands and Belgium, still have no legal requirements for parrot cages, whereas others, such as Germany and Switzerland, do.

In this case the authorities determine minimum measurements for caging and care of each parrot species. Any (potential) bird owner has to deal with the limitations of his house, garden or garage and has to make choices. Where will the African Grey live, how much of its existence can you expect the neighbours to tolerate, what is the easiest way to keep it clean, to what extent will the bird be part of the family, how many African Greys would you like to keep, etc.

The following housings are available for parrots:
• cage
• indoor aviary
• outdoor aviary with or without hut
• flight

Cage
Cages are available in many different colours, shapes and sizes. An African Grey living indoors needs at least a so-called jock cage. This is the absolute minimum and only appropriate if the bird can get out of its cage to exercise every day.

Things to look out for on a cage:
• Bars. Make sure that the bars can withstand the parrot's beak and run horizontally, so that the bird can climb on them. Also make sure that there are no

dangerous protruding parts, which could injure the bird.
- Feet. Cages can stand on wheels, on four feet or on a single foot. Choose a solid, reliable model and avoid dome cages. They are no good, as parrots like to climb. A square or rectangular cage offers far more opportunities to do so. A cage with four feet is much more stable than a cage with a single foot.
- Slide-out dish. An extractable dish is very useful when cleaning the cage.
- Perches. Perches which come with cages almost all have the same measurements. This might look orderly, but for the welfare of your bird you should replace these with natural sticks which you can cut to fit. These stimulate the bird's feet; it has to constantly readjust the bend of its feet rather than having them fixed in the same way all the time.
- Grid. Many cages have a grid at the bottom of the cage. Opinions about this vary strongly. Arguments in favour of a grid say that the bird's droppings and left-overs of the food fall through the grid which leaves the bird itself clean as it walks on the floor. Disadvantages are that it takes a lot of cleaning as things always get stuck on the bars, and it is also uncomfortable for the bird to walk on. It can also damage

its tailfeathers on the grid.
- Doors and openings. Some cages can be opened at the top. The roof is opened to both sides and a perch is placed between the two sides. This is an ideal observation post for your bird when it is allowed out of its cage.
- Positioning. Position an (indoor) cage on a quiet place, but so that your African Grey can still participate in family life. A parrot is prey in the wild and therefore prefers to have a wall behind it so that no 'threat' can come from there. A spot at the window is not normally advisable because of draughts and possible overheating in case the cage is next to a radiator or in the sun.

A home for your parrot

the right size. Indoor aviaries are also available in various colours, on wheels or with little feet, and they usually feature a slide-out tray for easy cleaning. You can also have an aviary made to your specifications. For the interior of the aviary, the same points as for the cage and the general points listed below apply.

Outdoor aviary

If you want to keep African Grey(s) in an outdoor aviary, you will again be faced with various designs and qualities. You can buy them ready-made, to assemble yourself, or you can build it yourself from scratch. Some important points you need to keep in mind:

- Many councils require planning permission for the building or you at least have to report it. Inform yourself about the regulations where you live. If you need planning permission, it is important to apply for it as soon as possible, so you can start the actual building when you planned to. When planning permission is required for an aviary, many councils first check in the neighbourhood to see whether there are any objections. You can, of course, ask the neighbours about their opinion yourself. This can prevent a lot of trouble later.
- Vermin in an outdoor aviary can cause a lot of problems. You can prevent this for example by laying good foundations under your aviary, and by not feeding

Indoor aviary

If you have enough room, an indoor aviary is ideal. It is room-high and square or rectangular. They are usually made of wire mesh. Make sure that the mesh is

the **African Grey Parrot**

outdoors if a hut is available.
- As our climate does not permit keeping parrots outdoors all year round, a hut is necessary in an outdoor aviary. Via a flap, the birds can decide whether to spend their time outside or inside. The flaps can be closed, so you can keep the birds inside in cold weather. Food and water and maybe the nesting boxes are in the hut.
- You can use any empty space in a shed, garage or part of the house, to which an outdoor aviary can be attached, as a hut. A connection to outdoors is established via holes for the birds to fly through.
- Always keep an eye on the temperature. A parrot's delicate parts, such as its claws, can easily freeze. A lot of birds enjoy staying outside in the cold, but a heated hut is essential so that they can warm up if it does get too cold outside. A heating (element) in the hut is a good solution.
- You can plant various plants, weeds and shrubs in the aviary. For advice on which plants are most suitable, we recommend that you read specialist books or consult your local garden centre.

Flight

A flight (an enormous aviary), in which the birds have enough space to fly longer distances and in which they can live in groups, is the closest approximation to a

natural situation. Unfortunately, most gardens are too small. This is therefore reserved for very few people, for zoos and bird parks. This subject will therefore not be covered in this book.

Suitable materials

Make sure that you use materials of good quality. African Greys need aviaries with a frame of (stainless) steel, zinced or galvanised material. These are preferable to wood, which is often chewed on straight away. If you do want to use wood, cover it with mesh to protect it.

Get information on the right size of mesh and attach it firmly to the wood with blind rivets. Feed and drink bowls can be attached in different ways: on a solid plateau in the cage or aviary, on a swivel platform or just hanging loose on the mesh. Bowls can be of plastic or stainless steel.

Bedding

Old newspapers and a layer of sawdust or shavings are suitable for a cage. Sawdust causes a lot of dust; shavings are not as dusty. You can also use newspapers, woodshavings and sawdust in an indoor aviary. You can use sand, soil or concrete for an outdoor aviary. Do not use shell sand.

Toys

Whether you are preparing a cage, an aviary or a flight for your

A home for your parrot

This parrot was sprayed with water

parrots, you will always need toys. Especially if an African Grey is kept on its own, it is important to pay attention to things to entertain it. All parrot species enjoy playing with toys, and anything put in the cage has to resist the destructive power of a parrot beak, and it must not contain poisonous substances.

Toys of good quality need not be expensive. A few thick ropes can quickly be turned into interesting climbing toys or swings. Empty toilet or kitchen rolls are brilliant for ripping apart, and walnuts are a great challenge if the bird has to crack them itself.

Secondhand homes

Cages and aviaries are generally quite expensive. They are, however, quite durable as long as they were a good investment in the first place. If you decide to buy a cage or an aviary secondhand, do not be tempted to put a bird in straight away, however clean it might seem. Disinfect the cage thoroughly with a solution from a pet shop. Afterwards, wash the cage thoroughly with water to get rid of all the remains of the (often very aggressive) disinfectant. Then you can prepare the cage for its new inhabitant. Always follow the instructions on the solution.

Feed and drink bowls

A cage or aviary also needs various bowls. They should be attached firmly. Bowls are needed for water, food, fruit and vegetables and possibly for stomach grit. All bowls need to be washed out daily.

If the air surrounding your parrot is very dry, you can offer it a separate bath. Most birds enjoy splashing around a bit. This is very good for their plumage. Most birds

the **African Grey Parrot**

also enjoy being sprayed with a plant sprayer or they might even enjoy a shower.

Twigs

All parrots like to be supplied with fresh twigs. Twigs of willow or of (unsprayed) fruit trees are ideal. They offer a brilliant distraction to the birds and the twigs are turned into small splinters in no time. Breeding birds will use the splinters as a supplement to their nesting box. The twigs moisten the air in the box, which aids the breeding process.

Nesting box

If you decide to buy a pair, you can add a nesting box to the interior. African Greys need a box measuring approximately 30 x 60 x 60 cm with an entry hole of approximately 12 cm diameter.

Nesting boxes can be made of wooden panels or of hollowed-out tree trunks. The latter look more natural in an aviary. Some birds might display a preference for a built nesting box, others for a hollow tree trunk. An inspection hole will allow you to check that hen, eggs and/or chicks are doing well. The lid or upper panel is normally detachable or hinged, which makes cleaning the box easier.

Once a breeding cycle has finished, take away the nesting box, clean it well and disinfect it

thoroughly. After that, the couple can have the box back. They often use it to sleep in together. You can take the box away for a few months, so that the birds do not start to breed again straight away. This will give them an 'obligatory rest'. There are, however, birds which will carry on laying eggs even without their nesting box. If they have to, they'll even lay eggs on the ground.

Domestic hazards

If your African Grey is part of the family, and obviously enjoying it, there will be quite a few perils lying in wait for it. They are often simple things, which people do not even think about, but which can be very dangerous for a bird. Think about hot pans on the oven, loose electric cables, doors being slammed, open windows, etc.

To eat is one of the most important things in your African Grey's life. Just as people, parrots have their own character and therefore their own particular likes and dislikes when it comes to food.

Every pet shop sells parrot foods. These include seed mixes, egg food, conditioning and rearing food, grit, buds, stomach gravel and 'sensible parrot treats'. The number of pellet foods has increased on the European market over the last few years.

Seed mixtures
Everybody knows the ready-made seed mixtures which can be bought in pet shops. One mix has more sunflower seeds, the other more peanuts. In any case, the

mixture contains seeds of various sizes, nuts and maybe peanuts. When choosing a mixture, the proportion of sunflower seeds is vital. Sunflower seeds are very fattening and have only very little nutritional value. You can raise the nutritional value of a mix with too many sunflower seeds by mixing in other seeds and nuts. You also need to be careful with peanuts in shells. These contain poisonous aflatoxins and are also very fattening. If you do want to feed peanuts, it is better to get the roasted ones intended for human consumption. They fulfil higher quality demands. They are still very fattening, though!

Pellets
With experience, from conversations with other parrot fans, reading and experimenting,

every owner will come to his or her own menu. There are alternatives, however. Some manufacturers have brought pellets for parrots onto the market. These pellets have been made by extrusion. Extreme heating (to about 200 degrees Celsius) makes these pellets free of bacteria and traces of agricultural toxins.

Pellets are most commonly accepted as food for chickens, pigeons, dogs, cats and horses. They are not yet very popular for parrots. Some manufacturers make pellets for all parrot species; others have different types of pellets - depending on the needs of a certain species or the time of year (resting or breeding time).

Advantages of pellets are:
• The bird gets the right amount of nutrients with each bite; Easy to feed even when someone else is looking after the bird; There is less mess;
• By feeding pellets which have been developed specifically for the African Grey Parrot, you can ensure that it will get calcium in the right ratio. This is very important for the development of your bird's bones.

Disadvantages of pellets are:
• Seem boring for the owner;
• The bird has less variety to choose from;
• Are not always easy to obtain (yet).

Everybody has to make his own decisions for his particular bird. Always be aware that your parrot is intelligent and has its own preferences. When given a bowl with various seeds and nuts, it will begin with the most fattening (read: tastiest) ingredients, and throw the rest out. When given new food regularly, it will only eat the tastiest, most fattening things. Anything you give your parrot must be in moderation and because it needs it. It does not matter if your bird has to empty its bowl, including the small, not quite as tasty, seeds. Those are usually the healthiest!

Pellets seem boring, but your bird should not seek distraction via its food. Attention from people around it, toys, tasks and other such things should provide distraction. Not the food, no matter what is in the bowl!

African Greys can be fed with pellets for African parrots every day, but they also need fresh fruit and vegetables and other supplements (see below) every day. The pellets will represent approximately 70% of their daily food.

Feed-related problems
Badly balanced feeding leads to abnormalities, poor condition and bad breeding results. Until a few years ago the parrot's real nutritional requirements had been

Pellets

Seed mixture for parrots

researched very little. This has thankfully changed in recent years. Parrot lovers can profit from this research. A good, healthy diet forms the basis of ideal care and therefore the animal's welfare.

Possible nutritional deficiencies which can be caused by a bad or unilateral diet:
- unstable protein balance, poorly adjusted protein levels, a lack of essential amino acids (lysine, methionine, etc.);
- insufficient vitamins (A, D, E, K, etc.);
- insufficient minerals (calcium, phosphorus, sodium, etc.);
- insufficient trace elements (iodine, manganese, selenium, etc.).

It does take quite a bit of time and experimenting (and asking) until you have found the right menu for your bird.

Calcium
African Greys are very sensitive to calcium deficiency. This shows itself in deformations of the limbs (bones) and in trouble related to eggs (difficult fertilization, deformed eggs or even totally stopping laying eggs). If there is a deficiency of calcium the body takes calcium from the bird's skeleton, which leads to osteoporosis. If a hen is to lay eggs, the body will have to extract more calcium from the bones, which leads to accelerated

osteoporosis. A breeding hen can therefore become ill quite quickly.

It is therefore very important to know the amount of calcium in your African Grey's feed and to adjust it to seasonal changes (breeding time or non-breeding time). If you use a seed mix as your main feed, you can add a calcium supplement. The same applies to vitamins and minerals. If you feed pellets as your main feed, then you do not normally have to add a supplement, as they have been designed to fulfil the nutritional requirements of the African Grey. This type of pellet will already have a slightly increased calcium level, which means that it would be dangerous to add even more calcium. Excess calcium can also lead to (serious) health problems. Therefore make sure that you read the feeding instructions for the pellets or ask the shop assistant for advice.

Other foods
Variety is very important when feeding. Besides products from pet shops and vets, there are plenty of every-day foods, which your parrot will enjoy.

Vegetables and fruit
Parrots are allowed all vegetables and fruit, apart from the very poisonous avocado. Apples, pears, carrots, paprika, lettuce, cabbage, broccoli or mango are all fine. Soft fruits, such as

bananas, mandarins, strawberries, cherries or grapes, probably do not cross your mind straight away, but most parrots love them. Rose hips are also popular. They grow wild in many places. You can freeze them and later defrost, wash and feed them to your birds throughout the year. The same applies to sweetcorn. Make sure that you do not collect rose hips and sweetcorn alongside a busy road, as they will be polluted. Do not be shocked if your bird passes red droppings after you fed it cherries or strawberries. This is caused by the fruit it ate earlier in the day. Many parrot owners have had quite a shock because of this.

Nuts

All parrots love nuts. Big macaws and cockatoos can crack a lot of nuts themselves. Smaller parrot species prefer it if you open the nuts for them. All nuts are suitable. Be aware of what I mentioned earlier about peanut shells and make sure that there is no mould on the nuts. By cracking the nuts, you can check the inside for mould and rot.

Hard-boiled eggs

You can feed your birds shelled hard-boiled eggs once a week, instead of ready-made egg food. Once a month they also get a bit of fresh garlic with their eggs. This seems to be an effective way of getting rid of any possible worms and is very healthy for the parrot.

The birds smell out of every pore for a few hours, but that is part of it.

Natural yogurt

This is (in a limited amount) good for the intestinal flora. If your birds find it too sour, you can mix in a banana or add a little syrup.

Muesli

Tasty with a little milk, yogurt or fruit juice. Your (modern) birds will also enjoy Kellog's 'Fruit 'n Fibre' with milk, yoghurt or cream cheese.

Sprouts

A number of seeds, pods and beans are suitable for sprouting. Put the seeds in a flat bowl with water to soften. Rinse them several times and let the seeds sprout on some damp kitchen roll for 24 hours.

As soon as small white and green sprouts become visible, you can feed them to your bird. Especially in the spring, this is an ideal addition for your birds, which are ready to breed. Softened seeds, pods and beans, which have been soaking in water, are also very popular.

Grit and stomach grit

Grit and stomach grit will help your bird's digestive system.

Besides food, your parrot must always have fresh drinking water.

Food and heat

It is important to change all soft food regularly on hot summer days to prevent mould. The cage also requires more attention than usual. Birds excrete a lot, and moulds and bacteria develop quicker in the heat. Mould will grow quite quickly in hot weather, especially on sprouts and soft

Sprouts

fruit. If you are not able to remove the bowls quickly, do not feed these items in very warm weather. It is also advisable to renew the water in your birds' drink bowls and baths more frequently when it is hot.

Chick feed

We do not support rearing chicks by hand. If it is not absolutely necessary, then rearing chicks by hand is not a good idea. An inexperienced enthusiast should not buy an African Grey which cannot eat by itself. Pet shops offer great baby food which will help a young African Grey to grow from its first day. These are powders to which you add boiled water and allow to cool. The gruel should be made very liquid for a very young chick, but with time it can be made thicker. All these manufactured feeds have detailed instructions with them. There are also breeders who have their own recipes with which they hand-rear chicks. This requires a lot of knowledge about the nutritional requirements of young parrots.

If you are not experienced in hand-rearing a parrot, do not be tempted to try. Buy your African Grey once it can eat by itself. This point has been made before, but it is very important. It also prevents a lot of trouble with spoilt babies, bent plastic containers and spouts, and chicks refusing to eat. A chick of twelve or thirteen weeks is also mentally much stronger and more able to cope with moving home than a five or six week old bird. A parrot is said to be independent when it is able to peel all its seeds, nuts, peanuts and other feedstuff, and when it can eat solid food. Baby food will not do any harm once in a while, but make sure you cut down on it quickly. Do not use the baby food as a means of 'bonding' with your young parrot. There are other ways of doing this: use the time you spend playing, teaching and generally interacting with your young grey friend.

What not to feed

Parrots do not eat or drink things such as (salty) crisps, chips, coffee, tea, alcohol and chocolate in the wild. Therefore feed your domesticated animals natural food for good health. The above items should never be fed, however much your bird would love to grab a pint!

It has also been discovered that parrots suffer a lot from nicotine. An endoscopic examination will show whether and to what extent the bird's air sacs have been damaged by nicotine. The less cigarettes are smoked around a bird, the better.

It is down to the individual owner to choose a menu for his darling(s). It is important that the focus remains on offering the bird a balanced diet. This is important if the parrot is to grow old in good health. As mentioned above: a good, healthy diet forms the basis for ideal care and therefore the welfare of your bird.

A parrot can become very old. Whether or not a parrot reaches the old age of thirty to forty depends on many factors.

Its diet, housing, hereditary disposition and luck play a role, of course. Health issues, too, need your attention if you want to enjoy your bird for a long time to come.

Acting
A bird will try to hide its condition for as long as possible, even from you. This is instinctive: a parrot cannot show that it is ill in the wild. It would be easy prey for its natural enemies. It has to and will stay with the group. This instinct is in every parrot, and it will try to appear as fit and healthy as possible in front of people too.

It is therefore important to observe your bird regularly when it is not watching you. You can then check whether there is anything wrong with it. Signs are crouching with raised feathers, panting, sitting on the ground instead of a perch, or excessive sleep.

Common illnesses
The following are some illnesses which (unfortunately) appear quite regularly:

Polyomavirus
This is a virus which is found worldwide and causes many problems in parrots and parakeets. Especially macaws, lovebirds, ring-necked parakeets, budgerigars and caiques are susceptible to it. The virus causes illness especially in young birds. The older the bird when infected,

the less serious the illness is. Grown birds often do not become ill when infected with Polyoma. They can, however, be carriers of the virus and therefore infect other birds unnoticed. Infection occurs when feeding their young or via material from their feathers and/or dried faeces.

Symptoms: slow growth process and slow emptying of the crop. A young bird is suspect if it shows bleeding under the skin or loses more than a drop of blood when it plucks a feather. Fledglings are suspect if the wing and tail feathers have not developed properly. They cannot fly and are called 'crawlers'.

Beak and Feather disease

This is a virus illness which is similar to AIDS in humans. Both illnesses attack the patient's immune system. Just as with AIDS, the virus of Beak and Feather disease can be in the system for years before the infected bird becomes ill. In the cases of both illnesses, patients might appear completely healthy again after three months. Both illnesses are also very difficult to treat. As Beak and Feather disease spreads via feathers and faeces, it is very important that an ill bird is recognised and isolated as quickly as possible.

Symptoms: it is often difficult to recognise this disease. Especially young birds die within a few days or weeks without showing the

feather abnormalities which are so typical of this disease. This form of the disease is particularly common with cockatoos and African Greys. Animals which become ill when the first feathers develop are affected straight away. This is often combined with vomiting, diarrhoea and lethargy. The beak and claws may also be affected. This usually starts with the upper beak. The horn becomes softer and lighter in colour and often splits; tumours develop, which can reach into the beak. The internal damage by this disease is much more serious than the outer symptoms. Many birds with Beak and Feather disease die within six to twelve months after the disease

manifested itself. They die of secondary infections, as their immune system is very weak. If the secondary infections are treatable, the bird may survive a long time.

The disease can be diagnosed by different methods. The most certain method is a blood test. There is, however, no vaccine available yet, although some promising research is being done in Australia.

Paramyxovirus

The family of Paramyxovirusses is very big and divided into nine groups. One virus from group 1 is called Newcastle Disease, is found worldwide and can affect many birds and mammals (including humans). Newcastle Disease has also been diagnosed in parrots. Especially cockatiels, amazons and parakeets are susceptible to this virus. The virus spreads via faeces and saliva and can damage various organs in the body. The symptoms are therefore manifold. Both young and old animals can become ill.
Symptoms: most ill animals show respiratory problems and diarrhoea. Some animals also show nervous symptoms (twisting the neck, trembling). These cases usually die, sometimes after months. If a bird does not show symptoms 30 days after being exposed to the virus (at a show, for example), the chance is very

small that it will actually become ill. The animal can carry the virus and infect others, however. Rosellas are particularly known for this. Vaccination is possible, but the law only allows it in exceptional cases. This means that the animal has to be in life-threatening condition. The vaccination gives protection lasting between a few months and a year. General hygiene and regular cleaning of the aviary with a chlorine solution help to kill the virus in the surroundings.

Paramyxovirusses of group 3 cause twisted neck syndrome. In African Greys, the virus can attack the pancreas. An increased excretion is a sign of this. The faeces can also be lighter in colour and greasy to putty-like in consistency. The mortality of animals with twisted neck syndrome varies. Newcastle Disease is far less common with parrots than twisted neck syndrome.

Psittacosis

This is caused by the bacterium *Chlamydia*. *Chlamydia* psittaci is highly contagious for many birds and mammals, such as horses, cattle, sheep, deer and humans, too. *Chlamydia psittaci* causes psittacosis, which is also called parrot disease. The disease is spread via feather material and dried faeces of ill birds.
Symptoms: the outer signs vary

with this disease, too. They include tightness of the chest, coughing, spitting, pus-like excretion from the nose, clamping tight an eye, light-green excretion of diarrhoea and yellow urates (granules in the urine). It often takes weeks before an infected animal displays symptoms. Parrots can also be carriers without suffering themselves. Infected parrots, ducks and chickens cause most, and the most serious, symptoms in humans. A human with psittacosis has flu-like symptoms, such as high temperature, serious headache, shivering, shortness of breath and drowsiness. If the illness is not recognised and treated, pneumonia, meningitis, liver and kidney damage can occur. Psittacosis is easy to treat with antibiotics. The treatment of a sick human or animal takes several weeks.

Zoonosis

Zoonoses are illnesses which can be transferred from animals to humans. Besides psittacosis there are more (bird) illnesses which can infect humans. They include salmonellosis, tuberculosis, camphylobacteriosis and influenza C. It would be too much to discuss all these illnesses in detail here. It is advisable though for you as a bird owner to bear in mind that you can catch diseases from your birds. This can be important information for your GP!

Sick bay

It is advisable to always have a 'medical cage' available in case you need to do some First Aid or a bird is obviously 'not quite right'. This does not have to be a major investment. A so-called guinea pig cage with a plastic upper and a hole, over which you can hang a 40 watt lamp, is sufficient. It does not need any perches, as by sitting on them an ill bird only wastes the energy which is so important for other things.

Put a lot of bowls with nice food and drink in the cage, which encourage it to eat and drink. Just put newspaper on the floor, so that you can easily check the faeces. Mix some honey or dextrose into the water. A high dosage of a vitamin A and B complex is ideal. If necessary, you might have to force-feed the patient via a crop catheter. This speeds up recovery. An infusion can be laid by the vet, as fluid is vital. Keep the bird as quiet as possible, so that it can recover.

Vets specialising in birds

The UK has a lot of very good vets, and an increasing number of them specialise in treating birds. They are always available if you need help, not just when your bird is ill or injured, but also for advice and tips concerning related issues, such as diet, caging and behaviour. It is always comforting to know that you can rely on a

specialist to help you with his expertise. If you have several parrots, it is often easier to ask the vet to come to your house to examine the birds, take blood samples, chip them or treat them however necessary. It can save your birds a lot of distress. A home visit is only an option, however, if the vet does not need any complex equipment or a sterile room.

Domestic dangers

The book "The Parrot", also from the About Pets series (ISBN 1-85279-206-X), contains a detailed list of the hazards which a pet bird can encounter in and around the house. These can vary from drowning in a toilet or a full bathtub to landing on a hot stove, inhaling nicotine or ingesting tin, tobacco, zinc, lead, etc.

Houseplants

Several plants contain poisonous substances, which can cause nasty illnesses or even be fatal. Poinsettias, for example, are poisonous, although a bird would have to eat quite a lot before it would be fatal. Poisonous (but often very popular) houseplants are, among others, all Diffenbachia species, oleander, goosefoot-plant, the great waxplant, the Strychnine Tree or Poison Nut (*Stychnos nuxvomica*) and the Small Periwinkle. Cacti are dangerous due to their spikes, which a bird can land on by

accident. Remove all poisonous plants before releasing your bird. Before buying new houseplants, inform yourself about whether they are poisonous to birds and possibly other pets.

Poisonous fruit

No bird should lack fruit and vegetables in its diet. There are very few fruits and vegetables which you should not feed, but never feed avocado. It is extremely poisonous for parrots!

Rest

It is paramount for a young African Grey's health that it gets plenty of rest, which is why we mention it here. Just as any young animal, a young African Grey spends a lot of time sleeping. New experiences, eating, playing, learning to fly and other activities take up a lot of the young bird's energy. So ensure that your young friend gets plenty of rest in its familiar surroundings: its own cage or its climbing tree. This allows it to re-energise and to work through all its new impressions.

Just as a young puppy, a young parrot will get more stamina as it grows older. Allow it plenty of time for this. A parrot does need attention, but not the whole day long. You will only end up with a hyperactive bird which cannot cope without attention.

Young, hand-raised
African Grey Parrot

Some breeders prefer to put couples together when they are very young. Others prefer to wait until the birds are three or four years old, when they are more mature.

When mature, parrots choose their partners because of their hormonal state. If they are being put together when they are too young, they are more likely to develop a brother-sister relationship than a mature male-female bond.

Putting a pair together
Putting a pair together is not easy. Parrots are very selective when choosing the partner with which they will spend the rest of their lives. African Greys are probably even more selective than other

species. The best option is if the birds can choose their partners from a group in an aviary or flight. Birds which are fond of each other will quickly sit on a perch together, sleep cosily next to each other or even choose a nesting box. It is then time to separate this pair from the rest of the group and put them in a separate aviary, of course with nesting opportunities.

If it is not possible to let the birds choose each other, then you will have to be sure about each bird's sex and give them the opportunity to get used to each other without rushing it. Put them in cages next to each other, for example, as this will allow them to see and hear each other. Observe how the birds behave towards each other and then put them together. It is advisable to do this on 'neutral

Breeding

the **African Grey Parrot**

ground'. This means that you should avoid the aviaries of the individual birds, as they view these as "their" territory. When placed in a cage or aviary which is new to both birds, then this is one less thing for them to argue about.

Determining the sex

It is almost impossible to determine an African Grey's sex by looking at it. Very experienced breeders can tell by the bird's head, but this means that you have to know your birds very well. For anyone else, an endoscopic examination or a DNA test will provide the necessary information.

During an endoscopy the bird will be given a general anaesthetic. Once the bird is asleep, the vet will make a very small incision into the bird's body, and then pass an endoscope through the hole. The advantage of this method is that it will not only allow you to see the bird's reproductive system, but also other organs. This is because the almost transparent air sacs in the bird's body make the organs clearly visible. This method therefore allows you to determine more than just the bird's sex. After the examination, which only lasts a few minutes, the bird will come round. The incision is sometimes stitched up, but this is not generally necessary, as it will usually heal by itself.

If you intend to have your bird's sex determined by a DNA test, the bird will not require anaesthetic. The vet will take some blood and send it to a specialist laboratory.

The advantages are:
- you can determine the bird's sex at a young age;
- the bird does not need anaesthetic;
- the blood can be tested for other things at the same time.

A DNA test is more expensive than an endoscopy, but it offers the advantage that the blood can be tested for other things at the same time and you can have it done at a young age. This is why this method is becoming increasingly popular. When buying a bird, it can provide the necessary certainty regarding issues such as (infectious) illnesses (see chapter 'Health') and it allows you to determine its sex before a purchase.

The breeding process

This book does not offer enough space to describe the breeding process in more detail. It is a beautiful experience to watch the parent birds prepare the nest, busy themselves with the eggs and later on look after their chicks.

Some statistics about the breeding process:

- African Greys lay on average two to four white eggs per nest.
- Intervals between eggs are one or two days.
- Only the hen broods.
- Eggs need to be incubated for approximately 28 days.
- The male bird feeds the hen while she is brooding. It also feeds the chicks later.
- Chicks leave the nest after 12 to 13 weeks.

Together with the vet you can choose the most suitable method of determining your bird's sex. Each method has its advantages and disadvantages and the age and condition of the bird are important factors.

Leave the chicks with the parents until they are at least ten weeks old. They take the best possible care of them, which will make the chicks strong and steady and ready to tackle the outside world when they are approximately ten to eleven weeks. They will not only be ready physically, but also mentally. The parent birds, too, enjoy fulfilling their natural roles. Ring the birds at the age of about three weeks with a solid ring of 11 mm diameter.

Rearing by hand

There is nothing more beautiful than watching adults rear their

chicks. Hand-rearing is a method for emergencies only. If something goes very wrong with parents and/or chicks in the nest, then you might have to make the decision to intervene and rear the chicks by hand. It must never be an end in itself. Chicks of ten to eleven weeks also become tame after two or three days of hand-rearing and are then suitable pets. If you decide to keep a pair and have never had any experience with rearing chicks by hand, then look for an experienced breeder in your area who will show you how to rear chicks and will let you help with his birds. This will give you experience in hand-rearing and will give you the opportunity to gain valuable tips in case it ever does become necessary with your birds.

Independence

A young African Grey is 'independent' when it is able to eat and drink by itself and is therefore no longer relying on baby food. This is usually after twelve weeks, although some chicks do need baby food once a day for another week. This is to ensure that they receive all the necessary nutrients. The bird does not only have to be able to eat soft fruit and similar things, but also to peel seeds and ingest hard fruit and nuts.

Only buy mature African Greys, so that you do not have to deal with baby food and all the other related

issues. Moving house is stressful enough for a young bird. It is therefore a big relief for both new owner and chick if the new family member is able to eat and drink by itself.

Besides all the things you can teach your pet, there are certain characteristics which come with each African Grey as 'standard equipment'. This genetic background is present in any individual, however tame.

Intelligence

Besides the natural behaviour (instincts), which each parrot has, you have to be aware of the following: an African Grey is simply intelligent! This may sound obvious, but it is something which you must be aware of. The owner of an African Grey has to bear in mind that he has a bird with the learning ability of a toddler. A child develops further and gradually becomes older, sensible and independent. The parrot remains

at the level of the toddler, but will need stimulation at this level for years to come. And you also have to take care of your parrot for the rest of its life. Looked at from this angle, looking after a parrot seems more difficult (or at least a longer process) than looking after a child. At least the child matures and will finally be able to look after itself.

Within its natural learning ability, the African Grey can learn a lot and develop quite far. You will be surprised how much this animal can learn and how quickly this will also lead to not-so-desirable behaviour. This is the other side of the coin: its intelligence enables the African Grey to figure out quite quickly how it can manipulate its environment and get its way by screaming, screeching and biting. It is down to the owner to try and avoid bad behaviour in the bird and to encourage good behaviour as far as possible. However, bad (and good) behaviour is always judged from a human perspective, as a bird thinks that screaming is great! It is natural for a bird to scream. The fact is that the African Grey is supposed to be part of the family, and as such has to adhere to certain rules. That does not mean growing up like a Spartan, but clear rules, a clear leader and on the other hand a lot of affection, play, happiness and safety.

Next to their need for safety, intelligence plays a major role in an African Grey's behaviour.

Remember that:
- Parrots have a reason for doing something (logic).
- Parrots want to be challenged with toys, chewing material, involvement in the family, and so on.
- Most parrots love to learn tricks, behaviour or words. They have, however, the concentration of a puppy, so do not make learning sessions too long or boring. Learning has to be fun.
- Parrots are just as keen to analyse and follow you as the other way round.
- Parrots can get confused when trying to understand too much. Keep signals, commands and other messages as simple and clear as possible.

It is the right combination between instincts and intelligence which makes parrots so charming and interesting. You must never forget, however, that they are tamed wild animals with certain characteristics. You have to recognize, acknowledge and appreciate them.

Learning ability
In parrots and other intelligent animals, a lot of the natural instincts have been replaced by the ability to learn. This allows them to adapt to changes in their environment and generally cope better with unknown situations.

Parrot chicks are very dependent on their parents, and they have to be shown everything in order to learn: from eating to mating. It is, however, their learning ability and the lack of certain instincts which have ensured that parrots have spread into the homes and hearts of people world-wide. Their learning ability also makes them

difficult pets, as these intelligent birds understand straight away if things go wrong. This results in various forms of stress behaviour.

Support

Especially as parrots are in principle an 'empty book' which has to be 'filled in' by the owner, it is important to buy a bird from a breeder/dealer who understands his own importance in the socialising process of the young bird. Breeders who understand the natural development of a young bird, and support it properly, produce birds which are happy, adapted and confident, and less likely to develop behavioural problems.

A young bird, just as a puppy or kitten, needs a good socialising period. This is the phase in which the young bird will need to gain as many new experiences as possible so that it will not become scared of the unknown.

A parrot in the house is an important family member and it needs plenty of love and attention. Never forget that there is always a group leader in the wild, and that you have to fulfil this role at home.

Natural behaviour

Although parrots do not react primarily instinctively, they are also not completely programmable. Their 'hard drive' contains already installed and permanent software.

The following is a list of fixed behavioural elements in the parrot genes. Instincts which each and every parrot has, and behaviour with which every owner can be confronted.

1. A parrot is prey

Every parrot knows this as soon as it crawls out of the egg. A parrot in captivity will react aggressively to all disturbances from above and behind it. Therefore always approach your parrot from the front and get young birds used to being picked up in a towel. Do not hang any mobiles or other things above the cage, even if they are out of the parrot's reach, and never put a bird under an open staircase, where it will be aware of things happening 'above' it. It is your duty to make sure that your bird feels safe, as this is the basis of a sound man-bird relationship.

2. A parrot experiences primarily visually

Parrots (as prey) have their eyes at the sides of their head, which makes their field of vision almost 360 degrees. They can see almost any predator approaching, whatever direction it is coming from. As each eye sees independently of the other, a parrot's vision does lose the sense of depth. This does not really matter however, as a parrot takes on a defensive position as soon as it sees an enemy approaching on the horizon.

Here are a few tips:
- Do not make unexpected, abrupt movements when near the bird.
- Do not place the cage, aviary and/or climbing tree next to a door or another spot where someone could 'suddenly' appear. The best place for your parrot is opposite a door.
- Make a sound when approaching your bird (loud footsteps are usually sufficient).
- Eye contact is very important for parrots. Eye contact with you will relax your bird. Look at it when you're vacuum cleaning, on the phone or similar.

3. The parrot is a gregarious animal

Parrots live in groups, as this offers protection. So it's important that you integrate a house bird into your 'group' and involve it in many aspects of family life. Birds see everyone in their direct environment as part of their group: family members, pets and sometimes even regular visitors. The rest does not count. A bird will not like everybody equally, but it will also not be easily panicked by a member of its group.

An adaptable, inquisitive parrot, which can accept new things, is

4. A parrot needs a leader

Animals which live in groups are genetically programmed to try and take over leadership once the present leader shows any signs of weakness. Although very little is known about the group life of the parrot, a few things are obvious. Many groups of parrots have guards which keep watch as the group forages for food. This is a very important function within the group which is indispensable. The guard is usually the bird sitting highest up in the tree, the one with the best and most unobstructed view. There is often a lot of squabbling and fighting associated with this function, which always goes to big, old and very experienced birds in the group.

less likely to be traumatised and will show a more developed curiosity and independence. New things may be toys and interior fittings of its cage or aviary, food, people, tasks and routines, but also your new hair colour or cut. As parrots develop, they go through different phases. There are times when they are more receptive to learning new things, for example what is safe and what is not. This is particularly true for young African Greys. During these learning phases they will also learn to accept changes and not to see them as an immediate threat. Once the bird is grown, this ability has to remain activated by regularly introducing your bird to new things. It keeps it adaptable and inquisitive and therefore less sensitive to stress.

This behaviour also influences the relationship with your pet in various ways. If your bird often sits on a higher spot than you in the house, it will assume that it has the top position and is boss. This is also why you should never let your bird sit on your shoulder. Take your bird onto your hand or lower arm. Teach it to climb on and off your hand on command. If your bird does not understand the command 'up', is in a mating mood, aggressive or irritated, never let it on your shoulder.

The above shows that parrots need rules. In the wild there are certain behaviours which are

accepted and some which are not accepted by the group. This has to be transferred to the domestic situation. The best example is a parrot which has not had its wings trimmed, and is allowed to fly through the whole house. This bird does not have to stay anywhere in particular, does not need you as a means of transport, and can make its own decisions. Of course it seems most natural to let the bird fly around like this, but you can make it a clear rule that it cannot sit and go wherever it wants. It is then only allowed to go anywhere with you as a leader. Trimming its wings therefore is one of the 'rules of the house'. This is, of course, no definite rule, and you can always choose something else.

5. Parrots are emotional and sensitive

Parrots recognise different moods and are very sensitive towards the energy flows and moods of the people around them. This is very important. It might happen that you feel like stroking your bird while it is really not in the mood. This is the difference between a parrot and a dog. Dogs are (generally) much milder and easier going. Even if you cannot easily see your parrot's mood, it will make this clear very quickly.

Your own mood, too, plays an important role. Parrots are very sensitive to it. If you are running late and try to put your bird back in its cage in a hurry, you will never succeed. Take a few deep breaths, approach your bird calmly and it will all be much easier. The more relaxed you are, the calmer your bird will be.

6. All birds are noisy

Vocal communication is very important for birds and other sociable animals. If you have a bird with considerable volume, expect to hear it on a regular basis. This does not mean that you should not stop it screaming for attention. But you should not try to stop natural behaviour such as the 'babble' at dawn and dusk and exuberant happiness when it greets you. It can be limited, but it must not be suppressed, as this causes resistance. A possible solution is to create a 'screaming hour'. At a time when it is convenient for you (and your neighbours) you can turn up the volume on your stereo and let your bird scream as much as it wants.

7. Bathing and showering are essential

Bathing and/or showering are essential for the physical and mental well-being of every parrot. A bird that does not want to shower, has not learned this, has not been reared in an environment encouraging curiosity and investigation, or has experienced a trauma later on. A bird is scared

by anything unfamiliar. Let it get used to a plant sprayer, a shallow bath, a tap or a shower. When drying it, make sure that your parrot is not exposed to draughts.

8. Parrots are active

In the wild, parrots are busy for hours flying, playing and chewing on twigs, trees, pods, fruit, seeds and anything else they can reach. They do this for both food and fun. In captivity, all they have to do is go to the feed bowl. It is therefore important to furnish a big cage or an aviary with various perches, toys and twigs to tear apart. Maybe you could also put

another play stand or climbing tree outside the cage. A Grey who does not play must learn to do so - for some reason it suppresses this natural behaviour, which is not good.

9. Parrots are mucky pups

Where parrots live becomes very obvious when you look at the floor. Pods, seeds, pieces of twigs and other things lie around. Parrots in the wild are one of the causes for new forest growth, as it is their 'task' to make a mess. It is in their genes. The mess is something you have to accept and can keep under control with a vacuum cleaner, mop and broom. Do not try to break this habit. Birds must be able to shred, crumble and spill their food as much as they like.

Talking

Parrots communicate with each other using their natural sounds. They warn and inform each other a lot and often. Some parrots are noisier at dawn and dusk, as these are the times when the members of the group gather together again in the wild. Wild African Greys have an extensive vocabulary: it ranges from soft whistling and clucking sounds to screeching as loud as possible. These sounds are used to tell other members of the group about something (the presence of food, danger, goodnight, I love you, etc.).

ey Parrot in a bird show at Bird
ntre Walsrode (D)

Communicating in captivity

A lot of African Greys in captivity (in the home or in an outside aviary) are known for their ability to talk and imitate. There are plenty of examples of birds who have conversations on the phone, sing Old Macdonald to the neighbourhood or give commands to the dog, who often obeys readily enough.

Sounds

Parrot fans who buy an African Grey because of its ability to talk often end up feeling cheated. By no means every Grey is a good talker. Even worse: Some will never utter a single word! They might prefer to imitate sounds, such as the bell of the microwave, the sound of the phone ringing, a door creaking, a dog barking or the doorbell. The sound will often be so perfectly imitated that the owner will end up going to the phone or the door, only to discover that the bird has fooled them once again.

The ability to talk depends on the individual bird, its desire to learn, its attachment to humans, its desire to 'belong' and how much work its owner is prepared to do to teach it. As parrots are very sociable animals, they will do anything they can to belong to their 'group'. And if this group consists of humans, they might feel obliged to learn their language. But the bird has to be able to do it.

My African Greys use not only their natural sounds to communicate with each other, but also human language. One of our males will reprimand another parrot with a sharp 'Bad boy' if he thinks the other parrot is too loud. He will even reprimand himself when he knows he is being up to mischief. Or he will even say it before he does something naughty, but this time with a mischievous glint in his eyes.

No guarantee

There is no guarantee that a young African Grey will ever learn to talk, whatever the vendor might say. If a Grey does learn to talk, it will normally start at an age of around a year. But here, too, there are exceptions. One of our chicks started talking when it was around three months old. No babble, but her own name nice and clearly. And now she talks her owners' ears off.

Other talkers

African Greys are not the only parrot species to produce talking individuals. A lot of amazons, too, can learn to talk very clearly and build up an extensive vocabulary. Some cockatoos learn to talk, but (like macaws) they will have a scratchier, more metallic voice. And parakeets can also occasionally learn to talk quite well.

Association

An African Grey's ability to associate (see the chapter on Intelligence) is very closely connected to how much talking ability it can develop. It will often say the right words at the right time and in a fitting situation. For example, 'Good morning' only when you enter in the morning and 'Good night' when the family goes to bed. This might seem very simple, but it is not. It just goes to prove how intelligent your parrot actually is.

Talking parrots can also often imitate several voices. An amazon that reprimands the dog with the father's deep voice may also imitate the happy voices of the children shortly afterwards. Spooky! Parrots therefore do not just say what we tell them to, but they generally know what to say, link certain words with certain situations and imitate voices of certain people. If they ever learn to talk, that is.

Playing and learning

What is true for all parrots is particularly true in the case of the African Grey: it needs constant stimulation, based on the fact that it has the learning ability of a toddler. This is why most Greys enjoy playing with you or learning tricks.

Different types of games

Useful games to play with your

Tips for teaching your bird to talk

- Start with short, clear words
- Always pronounce the word the same way
- Use the word in short sentences and let your parrot see what it means
- Always use the same words when leaving the room, going to bed, feeding your bird, etc.
- A lot of African Greys enjoy whistling and find it easy. Do not start with it at a young age, or your bird might stay 'stuck' in it. A few words first, then some singing and/or whistling
- Try not to swear in the presence of your bird. When swearing, words are often pronounced more clearly and with lots of emotion. A bird thinks this is great and swear words will therefore often be the first words it will imitate
- Keep lessons short, practise maybe one word or sentence and do not exceed a few minutes at a time
- End on a positive note: finish with an easy exercise or word so that you can praise your bird profusely and happily.

parrot are the common 'shell-game' in which the parrot has to tell under which cup its treat is, or solving a puzzle (for kids). Tricks such as laying 'dead' on its back, swinging very hard, walking over your head or waving with its foot are also very popular with most

African Grey with a Cockatiel

parrots. The bigger the audience, the more the bird will enjoy it.

A lot of African Greys (and other species) enjoy trips to the shops, the woods, the restaurant or will happily join you on a trip sitting on the handlebar of your bike. Make sure that the bird had its feathers trimmed (professionally) so that it cannot accidentally escape. Just as a dog, a parrot will enjoy going anywhere with you. It is obvious that it must be a 'sociable' bird who will not attack everyone in its vicinity or show other anti-social behaviour. Otherwise you will become very unpopular very quickly.

Tip

There are all sorts of books with games for dog owners. You can often adapt these games for your grey friend. Do not think that games are stupid. You will be surprised how much your bird enjoys doing something with you, exploring new things and being stimulated to learn.

The learning process

'Learning sessions' have to remain fun, both for the 'boss' and the bird. This is why they should never exceed 10 minutes (maximum). It is better to do something together a few times a day than for too long. In the latter case, the bird will lose its concentration, it will become moody and the effect will be lost.

Training is best conducted in so-called 'neutral' surroundings: surroundings where the bird does not normally live and where it cannot be distracted by all sorts of interesting things. A small room where the bird does not normally go and with as little distraction as possible is ideal. Choose one unit, game or trick which you want to practise. Build up the practice slowly and praise the bird profusely if it does something correctly. Even if it only makes an attempt at doing the right thing. It has to understand what you want it to do, and considering that it cannot understand you or see your intentions, that is very difficult.

Praise it with your voice (happy, high voice) or something nice (and preferably healthy) to eat.

Make treats as small as possible so that they do not totally mess up your bird's diet. Or take the treats out of your bird's daily amount of food. As soon as it understands a step you can go to the next part of the exercise. You can then decrease the amount of treats for all the in-between steps of the exercise, as the bird now has to do even more to receive its reward. As soon as the bird understands the whole exercise, you can use 'interval rewards', which means you do not reward it every time it did an exercise correctly, but only once in a while. The bird will have to guess whether and when it receives a reward. And a reward in the form of enthusiastic praise, a kiss or a cuddle counts too, of course. It does not always have to be food.

Training

Here is a short list of the most important things to remember when practising:

- Keep sessions short (max. 10 minutes).
- Use neutral surroundings.
- Work out what you want to practise before the session (one unit per training).
- Divide an exercise into small steps until you reach the goal.
- Associate the goal with a simple word as command.

- Reward your bird directly after a correct action (voice or a healthy treat).
- Keep treats as small as possible.
- While you are building up the exercise, decrease the size of treats for the previous steps.
- Always end on a positive note, praise your bird profusely, give it a final treat and leave the neutral space with it.

African Grey with Lovebirds

Toys in the cage

Your grey friend needs something to keep it busy. If there is no human company around, your bird will use some of the time to clean itself, sleep, eat and drink, but it will be left with some time to spare. Always make sure that it has toys in its cage, even if it seems frightened of the toy to start with. Try hanging it up differently or play with it yourself, without paying attention to the bird. Or try to make your bird jealous by playing intensively with the toy and make it clear that you are obviously enjoying it. Do not pay any attention to the parrot, but carry on playing. Finally you can ask it if it would like to play with the toy and after some attempts it will be so curious that it will want to try it.

Alex

Many African Grey fans know the work of American scientist Irene Pepperberg and her famous Grey Alex. Irene Pepperberg has been conducting experiments with Alex at the University of Arizona in the US since 1977. Alex was just a year old then and he has ever since participated in research to test the IQ of the African Grey. He can now distinguish colours and materials, count, ask for a treat, etc. His vocabulary consists of hundreds of words and he uses them at the right moment in the right context. Alex and three other research birds have taught science a lot about the mental ability of African Greys. What is even more important, however, is that the teaching methods which were successful with Alex also seem to work with mentally handicapped children. This means that learning programmes for this group can be continuously improved. Watching Alex and his mental abilities is a source of inspiration for all owners of African Greys – they find ideas for new games and challenges for their own birds. For more information, visit www.alexfoundation.org.

How to become a behavioural therapist for parrots

Our hectic society demands not only a lot from humans, but surely also from our pets. Parrots are no exception. To prepare pets as well as possible for life with humans it is vital to rear and socialise them well. Unfortunately, there are a lot of parrot owners who are not aware of the importance of raising their pet properly. And an incorrectly reared parrot is destined to develop behavioural disorders.

The course 'Behavioural therapy for parrots' offers a chance to professionally support parrots in their upbringing and socialisation and to cure behavioural disorders. The course consists of several modules and a period of work experience. If everything has been done to a satisfactory standard, you have the right to be awarded the certificate 'Behavioural therapist for parrots'.

The first module of this new course 'Behavioural therapy for parrots' is also available as a three day course to allow as many people as possible to increase their knowledge of species-specific behaviour, socialisation, learning principles and the raising of parrots. This course, which is open to anyone, is called 'Recognising and understanding the behaviour of parrots'. The following topics are dealt with over the three days:
- Popular species, their characteristic behaviour and the purchase
- Learning principles and their suitability when rearing parrots
- Species-specific behaviour of parrots and recognising their behaviour

- The development and socialisation of parrots
- Rearing and training parrots

You can choose to end the three day course with an exam. Only those candidates who pass the exam are allowed to carry on with the other modules, which will lead to a qualification as a behavioural therapist for parrots. You will find the contact address for this course in the chapter 'Useful Contacts'.

Useful contacts

The Parrot Society

This recognised charity was founded in November 1966 and from an initial membership of some 250 has grown steadily to its present international membership of over 6000.

Its aims are the study and conservation of all parrots and parrotlike birds other than the domestic budgerigar. The magazine is published monthly and is sent to all paying members, and is of interest to the beginner and more expert alike. Members are entitled to free, non-trade advertising in the magazine for wants, sales and exchanges of parrots; council members and Officers are elected by ballot and are responsible for the proper running of the Society.

The Parrot Society is eager to help the beginner and has published five booklets on different parrots and parakeets.

The Parrot Society

92A High Street,
Berkhamsted, Herts, England,
HP4 2BL, UK
Tel: (44)(0) 1442 872245
Fax: (44)(0) 1442 872245
www.theparrotsocietyuk.org
E-Mail:
les.rance@theparrotsocietyuk.org

The National Council for Aviculture

Administrator
4 Haven Crescent
Werrington, Stoke on Trent,
Staffs. ST9 0EY.
Tel: +44 (0)1782-305042
Fax: +44 (0)1782-305042

Department for Environment,
Food and Rural Affairs (Defra)
UK's CITES Management
Authority
Global Wildlife Division - Defra
1/17 Temple Quay House
2 The Square
Temple Quay
Bristol BS1 6EB
United Kingdom
Tel: +44 (0)117 372 8749
Fax: +44 (0)117 372 8206
E-Mail:
wildlife.licensing@defra.gsi.gov.uk

World Parrot Trust
The World Parrot Trust has
thousands of members in over 50
countries. Their branches work to
achieve the stated aims of the
World Parrot Trust, which are:
The survival of parrot species in
the wild, and the welfare of
captive birds everywhere.

Administrator,
Glanmor House,
Hayle, Cornwall TR27 4HB
Voice: +44 (0) 1736 751026
Fax: +44 (0) 1736 751028
Administrator Email:
uk@worldparrottrust.org
www.worldparrottrust.org

The Parrot Society of Australia
C/o Dave Johnson
P.O. box 75
Salisbury
Qld 4107
Australia

Pakara
Major Parrot Society in the
Netherlands
Administrator
Stationsweg 5a
2445 AH Aarlanderveen
The Netherlands
Tel. (0031) 0172 - 572096
E-mail: penningmeester@pakara.nl
www.pakara.nl

Country of origin:	Africa
Habitat:	Woods, mangroves, savannas and agricultural areas
Sub-species:	Congo Grey Parrot and Timneh Grey Parrot
Height:	36 cm
Sexual maturity:	At 4 to 5 years
Number of eggs:	2 to 4 white eggs
Fledge:	12 to 13 weeks
Hatch:	After 28 to 30 days
Characteristics:	Intelligent, talent for speaking
Life expectancy:	70 years or more

The African Grey Parrot

the **African Grey Parrot**